Cache Creek

Cache Creek

A Trailside Guide
to
Jackson Hole's Backyard Wilderness

SUSAN MARSH

Sastrugi Press

San Diego • Jackson Hole

Sastrugi Press / Published by arrangement with the author

Cache Creek: A Trailguide to Jackson Hole's Backyard Wilderness

The author has made every effort to accurately describe the locations contained in this work. Travel to some locations in this book may be hazardous. The publisher has no control over and does not assume any responsibility for author or third-party websites or their content describing these locations, how to travel there, nor how to do it safely. Sketch maps provided are approximate. Refer to official Bridger-Teton National Forest maps.

Any person exploring to these locations is personally responsible for checking local conditions prior to departure. You are responsible for your own actions and decisions. The information contained in this work is based solely on the author's research at the time of publication and may not be accurate. Neither the publisher nor the author assumes any liability for anyone exploring, visiting, or traveling the locations described in this work.

Sastrugi Press
2907 Iris Avenue, San Diego, CA 92173, United States
PO Box 1297, Jackson, WY 83001, United States
www.sastrugipress.com
Quantity sales: Special discounts are available on quantity purchases by corporations, associations, and others. For details, contact the publisher at the address above.

Library of Congress Catalog-in-Publication Data
Library of Congress Control Number: 2016938520
Marsh, Susan
Cache Creek / Susan Marsh - 1st United States edition
p. cm.
1. Nature-Regional 2. Women authors 3. Nature-Plants 4. Travel
Summary: Cache Creek: A Trailguide to Jackson Hole's Backyard Wilderness portrays the essence of a place, with an emphasis on natural and human history, ecology and features that can be experienced from the main trail system.
ISBN-13: 978-1-944986-02-5
ISBN-10: 1-944986-02-2

508.4—dc23

Printed in the United States of America

All photography, maps and artwork by the author, except as noted.

10 9 8 7 6 5 4 3 2 1

Contents

ACKNOWLEDGMENTS

For the five years it took to complete this book, I was encouraged by friends, natural resource professionals, patient companions who waited while I composed photographs, and fellow writers. Thanks to all.

Sincere thanks to those who read the early manuscript and gave me valuable feedback: Beverly Boynton, an accomplished climber and river runner whose curiosity and enthusiasm for all things wild never fails to inspire me; Linda Merigliano, Forest Service recreation and wilderness management guru who gave much encouragement and assistance; and Frances Clark, professional botanist who provided extensive comments on the manuscript.

Much credit goes to Kathy Springmeyer at Sweetgrass Books in Helena, Montana, who taught me the fundamentals of preparing a book like this for publication. Finally, thanks to Aaron Linsdau of Sastrugi Press, for bringing it forth into the world.

Map to Cache Creek

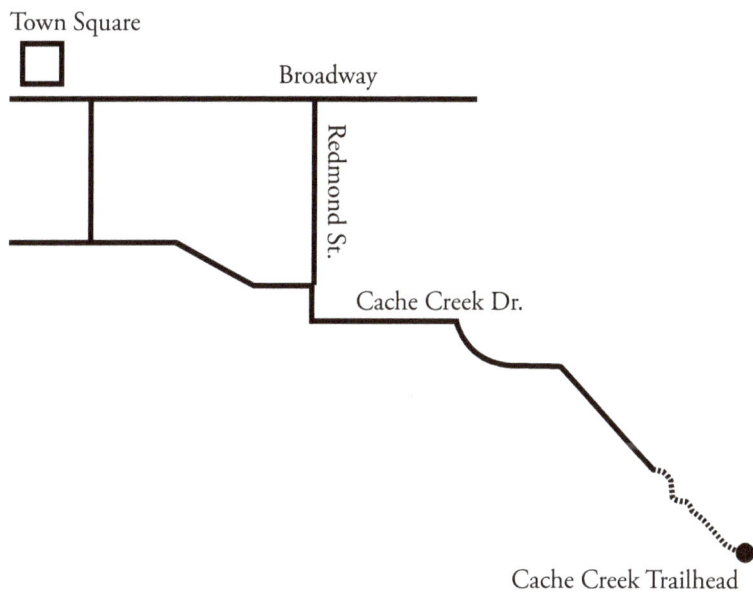

Town Square

Broadway

Redmond St.

Cache Creek Dr.

Cache Creek Trailhead

DID YOU EVER WONDER...

⋄ Where you can take a short, scenic hike close to town?

⋄ Why there are forests on one side of a valley and sagebrush on the other?

⋄ Why elegant jewel-clad butterflies eat poop?

If so, this book is your go-to resource. Five minutes from the hubbub of Jackson's town square, Cache Creek offers the chance to immerse ourselves in wild nature. It's a place where you can see how the world works, and *Cache Creek: A Trailside Guide to Jackson Hole's Backyard Wilderness* shares some of the ways you can do it. No experience needed: bring your attention and a few hours of your time. You will be enchanted.

It is not necessary to be an expert to encounter a place with open eyes and an open heart, and a dash of curiosity. In fact, it might be better if you're not an expert. Instead of saying, "Oh yeah, that's a Western Tanager singing," and continuing on with a satisfied march, you might say, "Hmm, I've never heard that before. It sounds a little like a robin…"

You might stop long enough to listen to the song again, and say to yourself, "For sure, not a robin." If you're lucky the bird will show himself. He's flashy, almost tropical, with bright yellow and scarlet. He is a bird you will never forget.

You don't need to know that he is a male Western Tanager (but if you knew that he eats yellow jackets, you might tell him thanks). You saw him in all his brilliance. You heard him sing. You were granted a glimpse into his world, and it is those brief glimpses that open a window for much more.

Susan Marsh

Western Tanager.

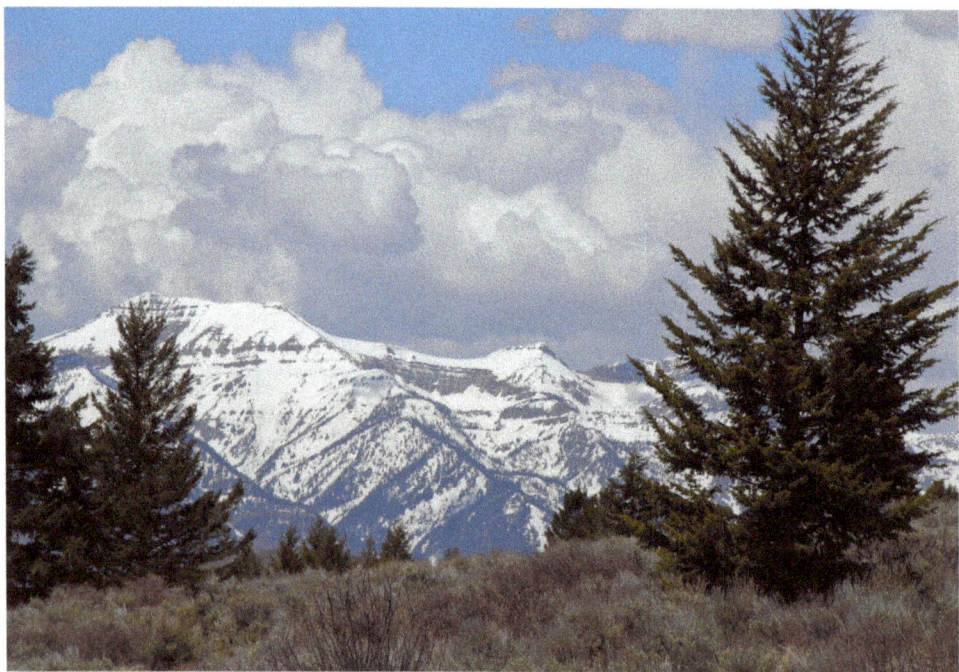

View to Rendezvous Mountain from one of the lower trails in Cache Creek.

Part I: This Special Place

What's So Great about Cache Creek?

Here's what some of the locals have to say about it.

"I love the view coming down the Hagen Trail across to the Tetons."

"Hiking and skiing with my dog."

"I love the arrowleaf balsamroot in the early summer!"

"It's where I learned to cross-country ski."

"Cache Creek made such an impression on me 30 years ago that I used it as it as my 'visualization' for getting me through labor. It has seen many changes through the years but it has maintained its special place in my heart."

"My favorite thing is skiing up Cache Creek. I particularly love getting past the normal lunchtime turnaround as the trail drops down into the trees."

"Hiking in the spring after snowmelt and heading over to Game Creek."

"I love the northeast facing slopes that have a mix of thick young Douglas-fir and old bug-infested patches. You can tell where the fire in the late 1800's burned."

"Gary Snyder once wrote that you have to know your watershed. Well, Cache Creek is my watershed."

How To Get There

The photo above, of Jackson from one of the Cache Creek trails, shows the close proximity of this area to town. To reach Cache Creek from the Town Square, head east on Broadway, drive 6 blocks to Redmond Street, and turn right onto Redmond (across from the hospital). Go 5 blocks on Redmond to where it starts up the hill and take a left onto Cache Creek Drive. This street will take you directly to the main trailhead, about 1.2 miles away.

Once you arrive...

   The main trailhead is shown on the sketch below, along with some secondary parking spots that may be confusing. If you are visiting for the first time, it's easiest to use the large parking area shown and head directly east from there, where you will see a gate across the road. This is the Cache Creek Trail. There is an information board with a map showing the various trails.

From the far reaches of the Cache Creek watershed (fire-weed on the divide with Horse Creek, above) to the lower end of Woods Canyon near the trailhead (lifting fog on a late October morning, right), Cache Creek offers an amazing diversity of habitats, elevation range, and opportunities for exploration.

What Waits for You

Rest. Wander. Enjoy. Go home refreshed. The attention we pay can take the form of bird watching, identifying wildflowers, noticing the caress of a warm breeze or the quiet of natural sounds.

Being present and aware of what surrounds us can inspire a photo, a poem, a scribble in a notebook. It invites contemplative strolling, slowing down, and allowing the persistent fidgeting of the mind to quiet for a while. Some of us might even be silly enough to lie belly-down in the grass for a bug's-eye view of the earth we cherish.

A place for quiet contemplation

You may be saying, "Huh?" Cache Creek on a summer (or winter) weekend afternoon might best be described as "a zoo." Between the parking lot festivities, covered wagon rides, and dozens of hikers and bikers, Cache Creek can hardly be called a sleepy getaway. While it offers a place to play along its considerable network of trails, one can also find something more: the chance to slow down, be quiet, and pay attention.

Opening to the natural world is something that happens without effort. In fact, someone for whom Cache Creek may be new could have more 'wow' moments than a frequent visitor. There is that little kid in all of us who still yearns for wow moments, who pulls at our sleeves as we walk along, saying, "Hey—look at that! Caterpillars."

Caterpillars? Yuck. But what if we look past our initial ingrained revulsion? Western tent caterpillars, the larvae of an inconspicuous fuzzy brown moth, are more than meet the eye. A bit of research about these guys may have you agreeing with the kid who says, "wow."

Consider the communal tent. As with all real estate in Jackson Hole, location matters. It starts in the crook of a small branch (near their favorite food, young leaves), where it catches the early morning sun. The position of the tent is critical because the caterpillars need the sun to elevate their body temperatures. A cold caterpillar can't digest its breakfast.

In addition to location, design is important. The caterpillar tent consists of discrete layers of silk separated by gaps, like rooms in a house. The temperature in these compartments varies, so the caterpillars can adjust their body temperatures by moving from one compartment to another. On cool mornings they gather into a tight bunch just under the sunlit surface of the tent, where the temperature can be over 50°F warmer than the surrounding air. Talk about the greenhouse effect.

Western tent caterpillars seem to prefer members of the rose family, especially chokecherry. They also relish antelope bitterbrush and Saskatoon serviceberry.

A place to learn and wonder...

Tent caterpillars emerging with the leaves.

Tent caterpillars have their place in the larger scheme. When the host plant is defoliated, the ground below finds increased sunlight which gives a boost to smaller plants or seedlings.

The eaten leaves pass through the caterpillars to emerge as little pellets which return nutrients to the forest floor. The moth pupae provide nutritious meals for small mammals, and the adult moths are eaten by birds and bats.

In June the caterpillars disperse and the shrubs that hosted them are left to recover. While some branches may die completely, plants that evolved with such disturbance have become experts at sprouting later.

If that's more than anyone wanted to know about tent caterpillars, be assured that most of the wonders of nature covered in this book have to do with wildflowers, birds, trees, and water. Easier on the eye, and sometimes—like the tent caterpillars—so familiar we fail to notice.

DID YOU KNOW? Cache Creek was named by early settlers for thieves who cached their booty at a ranch beside the creek. "Cache" is a common term in the region for any goods or gear stored in the woods for later retrieval—a term reminiscent of the early fur trapping era.

A Two-minute Geologic History

Cache Creek lies at the edge of the Gros Ventre Range, part of the physiographic province known as the Middle Rocky Mountains. The creek springs from the confluence of several streams near the base of 10,304-foot Cache Peak and runs for about six miles down a deep, narrow canyon into the town of Jackson. The geologic sequence in Cache Creek includes nearly every named formation known in the Gros Ventre Range.

The most ancient rocks are shales and limestones over 500 million years old. Above these lie a sequence of limestone, dolomite, shale, and sandstone. Together they represent hundreds of millions of years in earth history. Hiking the trails when they are wet is a good way to identify certain geologic strata, including the Triassic Chugwater Formation and the Jurassic Sundance Formation. You know you've found these when the trail is super greasy and six inches of mud clings to your boots.

"Younger" rocks (205–65 million years old) are represented mostly by shale and sandstone. The Cretaceous Sohare and Bacon Ridge Formations contain coal that was mined in upper Cache Creek in the early twentieth century.

Zebra-striped chert.

The relief in Cache Creek canyon results from folding and faulting of the sedimentary rocks, and corresponding uplift. A large part of the terrain is covered by landslide debris. Glaciers once occupied the valley, but the rocks they covered have been subject to more recent land movement and water-related erosion, muting the visible effects of glaciation. There are no glaciers within the watershed today.

Did you know? Fossils found in some of the rocks in Cache Creek include corals, brachiopods and other marine animals from the Madison Formation. The top (youngest) part of the Madison Formation, called the Bull Ridge Member, contains unusual zebra-striped chert.

Alpha pika of the Woods
Canyon talus slope

"There's my hay pile!"

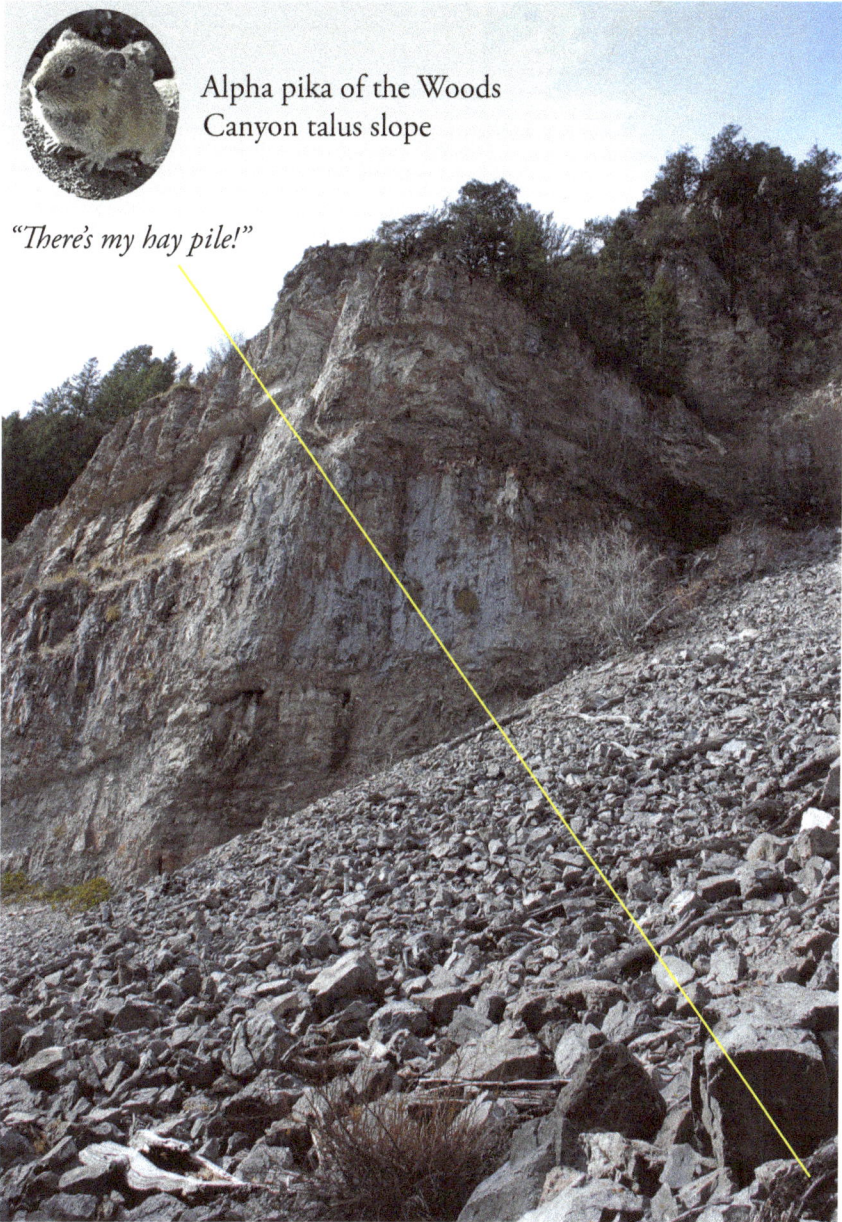

For those wanting to see some "real" bedrock, a short side trip up Woods Canyon yields views of tall limestone cliffs and their talus, part of the Madison Formation.

So, are these fossils?

These little white shells along the trail are the remains of a living land snail of the genus Oreohelix. It's rare to find a live one since they live under leaf litter or in the ground, and unless it's very wet they come out mostly at night.

These small terrestrial gastropods need shelter, moisture, food, and calcium carbonate (to make shells). Cache Creek, with lots of dissolved carbonate in the soil from limestone and dolomite, is ideal for them. Members of this genus are found where similar conditions exist, so they are among the more common of the land-dwelling members of the snail family.

Part of nature's clean-up crew, these little guys eat whatever they find on the ground. Without them we'd be knee-deep in leaf litter, miscellaneous dead stuff, and tent caterpillar scat.

Don't step on me!

Cool Fact: Oreohelix is unique among Rocky Mountain land snails. It doesn't simply lay its eggs and creep away. The young hatch internally and can be retained inside the adult for some time as they begin to grow. They are born live, complete with small shells. This strategy is an adaptation to the dry rocky slopes where the snails live.

They Who Share This Place

Though right on the edge of town, Cache Creek is vibrant with wildlife. The diversity of habitats invites forest creatures such as red squirrels and pine martens, brush-browsing moose and deer, and grazers such as elk. Bighorn sheep may be seen in winter in lower slopes near Crystal Butte.

Woods Canyon harbors pikas, usually seen at higher elevations, but the deep blocky talus in the narrow canyon offers enough protection from summer heat that these diminutive members of the rabbit family can survive here. Pikas are usually found among the talus slopes at the upper reaches of Cache Creek.

Top predators show up in the watershed as well, often in winter when prey species are concentrated at lower elevations. Mountain lions, coyotes, gray wolves, golden eagles, and even a set of wolverine tracks have been spotted in Cache Creek. Black bears seek berries, carpenter ant larvae in rotten logs, and the cambium layer of lodgepole pine trees. Grizzlies wander through on occasion.

Resident and migratory birds and mammals make use of every available habitat, depending on the time of year: black bears will break many branches in search of ripe serviceberries in the fall. Elk find windblown grass for winter forage. Coyotes (below) and ermines hunt for rodents under the snow.

In spring, Red-tailed Hawks arrive as voles, ground squirrels and least chipmunks begin their reproductive cycles. The diverse riparian and shrub habitats invite many songbirds to nest and forage in Cache Creek. Ravens, Clark's Nutcrackers, Steller's Jays, and American Crows keep things lively with their loud announcements.

Cache Creek is a special place to us, but it is good to remember that for the wildlife, it is home. Like courteous guests in someone else's house, we need to give them space and respect their needs. We are privileged to share the trails with them, for seeing any creature living undisturbed in its wild habitat is a treat to savor.

Did you know? Cache Creek lies within the vast Bridger-Teton National Forest. One of the largest in the lower 48, this national forest is over 3.4 million acres, or 5310 square miles. Cache Creek's part of the forest is only 11 square miles.

D🐾GS

The most common 'wild creature' seen along the trails

One of the things people appreciate most about Cache Creek is that it's a great place to exercise and socialize canine family members. It's doubtful, however, that the people appreciate it as much as the dogs do.

Thanks to PAWS of Jackson Hole for providing convenient dog-poop bags (aka Cache Creek hand warmers) and a place to dispose of them, for clean water and trails.

A stroll through the seasons in Cache Creek

Winter

When Water Plays

H_2O is the world's #1 miracle compound. It is a mineral that can exist in three states at the earth's surface temperatures: gas, liquid, or solid.

In its solid form, it can be crystalline or globular, brittle or plastic, able to flow and drape luxuriantly.

Throw a rock into Cache Creek and it sinks. Ice floats. This attribute of water allows for many forms of aquatic life that would not exist if ice acted like the other the natural compounds that we call rocks.

A reversal of the usual ice-on-top rule occurs during periods of extreme cold. Cache Creek is perfect for the formation of anchor ice, which forms on the bottom of the creek bed. Fast-forming crystals of frazil adhere to each other and to the stream's rocks and build into masses that act as dams. The creek backs up behind them and water flows over the ice, as shown here at the "dog pond." In addition to raising the level of the water, anchor ice restricts flow and volume.

As ice freezes to the creek banks, shelves of aufeis result, elevated and often multi-layered with pockets of air between them.

For most of the winter, the creek's mantle of ice can't decide if it's coming or going. The cycle of freeze-up, melting, and later re-freezing makes for an ever-changing creekscape of ice formations.

Winter arrives in early December most years, and hangs on for months. No groundhogs announce the day when it's half over, though rodents such as least chipmunks and Uinta ground squirrels make their appearance by early March.

Everyone in Jackson Hole has his or her personal marker for the end of winter: by Valentine's Day, the sun actually shines on the slopes at Snow King. A patch of bare ground appears at the edge of the lawn. The song of a Red-winged Blackbird can be heard from the National Elk Refuge. No matter which sign of spring each person notices, we are all elated when it comes. Yet, we hate to bid farewell to the lovely winter season.

Let Us Now Praise… Mud Season

Early spring has unique and overlooked charms for the few Jackson Hole residents who stick around. You have to be patient, observe closely, and bring waterproof boots and a raincoat. As winter slowly opens into spring, the miracle of life reborn each year is on display.

First flowers of the season: quaking aspen. White fuzzy globes appear as the protective scales open. Several weeks pass from the pussy-willow stage to fully open staminate catkins (left). Birds and insects flock to the rich pollen source. When the catkins dry and fall away, it's almost leaf-time.

Along the creek, thinleaf alder is another early bloomer, with catkins dangling from the twigs like fancy earrings. By the end of April, bog birch and some of the willows will join the bloom.

Did you know? Some of the oldest remaining buildings in Jackson are made from logs that came from Cache Creek. Old stumps and the remains of roads and skid trails are still visible along some of the forested trails. In 1942 the drainage was closed to timbering to protect Jackson's culinary water supply, which came directly from the creek.

When the snow melts from the side of the trail and the first evergreen leaves appear, it's an event worth celebrating. Among the few evergreen shrubs in Cache Creek are two of the most common, shown on this page.

Mountain lover (right) is related to the ornamental boxwood. It has finely toothed, glossy leaves arranged opposite to one another along the stem. It is an understory shrub in forested areas, but also grows in the open.

Oregon grape (below) belongs to the barberry family. It grows close to the ground with thick leathery leaves resembling holly. As soon as the ground warms, the fragrant yellow blooms begin to form.

Buds will appear in long panicles above the leaves of Oregon grape before the end of April. The tiny pink flowers of the mountain lover start to bloom in mid-May.

Long before either of these low-growing shrubs blooms, each cheers the early spring wanderer with the first taste of greenery on the forest floor.

WHAT IS THIS STUFF?

A familiar sight to early-season wanderers, it forms an intricate web that appears as the snow melts. It is a fungus known as alpine snow mold. Most fungi threads (mycelia) inhabit the upper horizon of the forest soil, but this one lives between the ground surface and the snow.

Alpine snow mold needs temperatures close to freezing and very moist conditions to grow and reproduce. Ideal conditions are fleeting, so early spring is the only time this mold covers the ground surface in its delicate lacy mat. As soon as the snow is gone, so is the mold—except for next year's spores.

What does snow mold do? A nutrient flush takes place with snowmelt, allowing the mold to grow rapidly. It is thought to contribute to the flux of stored carbon dioxide from the soil. It metabolizes forest litter and makes use of sugars released by conifers in late winter. In common with other forest soil microorganisms, alpine snow mold breaks down complex compounds and helps make nutrients more available to plants.

25

SPRING

Green bog orchid.

Runoff

Spring means snowmelt and high water. Cache Creek turns muddy and green-brown, but it doesn't last long.

The U.S. Geological Survey stream gauge has been measuring flows in Cache Creek since 1963. 1971 saw a rare "100-year" flood, with Cache Creek peaking on June 24 at 225 cubic feet per second (cfs), twenty times the annual average flow. Not much flooding occurred, except at the north end of town, where people were seen canoeing past the Bridger-Teton National Forest headquarters building.

Even though the watershed of Cache Creek has considerable erosive soil, the usual creek runoff color doesn't look like tomato bisque or café latte, the way it does in other nearby rivers. Cache Creek is mildly turbid from overland flow and the contribution of several small tributaries, and it soon clears up after the main flush of snowmelt. Brief periods of greater turbidity usually mean that a chunk of the stream bank or landslide debris has entered the water somewhere upstream.

Did you know? Jackson's first electricity came from a dam on Cache Creek, with a small hydropower plant operated through the 1920s at what is now Mike Yokel Park.

Above: Cache Creek in late fall. Below: the same spot at peak flow near the end of May.

Clockwise from upper left:
sticky geranium, milkvetch,
low larkspur, sidebells
pyrola, common twinpod.
Arrowleaf balsamroot at
center.

…And First Flowers

IT'S A DELIGHT to recognize favorite plants by their leaves, and a delight to see them opening when the sun warms the earth. Some are simple, others are compound, made of leaflets arranged in particular ways. Some are plain while others are deeply cleft, toothed, or lobed. Some are opposite each other on the stem, while others alternate up the stem. Some form a basal rosette on the ground. Imagine any shape for a leaf, and chances are you can find something like it in Cache Creek.

The first wildflowers to appear are so tiny you have to search for them, except for the showy buttercups. These early bloomers set seed and go dormant before the taller wildflowers can shade them out. The energy they gather from a few weeks of spring sun is enough to sustain these little plants underground for the rest of the year.

Cache Creek has two species of early spring buttercup: sagebrush buttercup (at left) and Utah (or Jove's) buttercup (below right).

Sagebrush buttercup blooms in open areas. Its petals are short and roundish, or may be lacking. Leaves are wide and pointed at the end, and veins are usually obvious. Some of its leaves have lobes.

Utah buttercup has more slender petals, and its leaves are deeply lobed into three. The three-part lobe is a common leaf form in buttercups, whose botanical name Ranunculus is taken from the Latin word for frog, rana. The leaves are thought to resemble a frog's foot.

SUMMER

Leopard lily.

"If Cache Creek was anyplace be-sides Jackson Hole, it would be a national park."

...an out-of-town friend, on walking up the Cache Creek Trail for the first time.

A Summer Stroll

The main Cache Creek Trail was a road for most of its long life, beginning as an access route for timber cutting and coal mines. In 1994 the road was closed to traffic and the existing trailhead parking areas were built.

This road is now the most popular of the trails in Cache Creek, hosting several hundred people on peak days. Still, it's possible to stay in the slow lane and enjoy the colorful birds and wildflowers without having to dodge faster-moving traffic.

The lower trail passes a streamside zone where riparian vegetation dominates. Topography limits this zone to a narrow strip, but it serves its function of dissipating stream energy and creating a diverse habitat. Red-twig dogwood, thin-leaf alder, northern black gooseberry and several species of willow thrive there.

Uncommon orchids (yellow spotted coralroot, above) and violets (the tiny marsh violet, opposite page) find a home in the springs and bogs near the creek. The sound of running water is never far away, a peaceful counterpoint to the intense activity of a typical summer in Jackson Hole.

Cache Creek is inviting and peaceful in summer. The water is cold, but that doesn't stop dogs, children and a few adventurous adults from enjoying a dip.

Cache Creek's clear, cold water runs over rocks like a serenity fountain meant to lower stress. The effect is the same.

In mid-summer, Cache Creek is gin-clear and infused with sunlight. Rocks shine through with a mix of ocher and deep brick red. For the moment in time we call August, the natural world seems to take a breath and let it out in a long slow sigh of satisfaction, the tasks of growth and raising young now past, preparations for winter yet to come. Cache Creek is a place of refuge for people whose hectic summer schedules have gotten out of control.

A Wildflower Interlude: Daisy or Aster?

Wildflower lovers are often confounded by the aster family. With so many showy members of this group in Cache Creek, a few hints for sorting them out may be helpful. These sketches distinguish members of the daisy (or fleabane) group from the several genera included within the asters.

DAISY

Ray flowers (the ones that look like petals) are numerous and narrow.

Green bracts under the flower are long and thin, all the same length, and usually arranged in a single row.

Ray flowers fewer and often wider than daisies.

ASTER

Bracts under the flower are wide, short and arranged in 3 or more imbricate layers like shingles.

Big yellow sunflowers are difficult to distinguish if you only pay attention to the flower. Look for leaf shape and plant habit to tell them apart.

Right: Arrowleaf balsamroot. Leaves are shaped like arrowheads, broad at the base, pointed at the tip. All are basal (none on stems) and silver-haired.

Below: Two members of the genus Helianthella. Lower left is little sunflower. Leaves are opposite on the stem, flowers form a broad cup raised at an angle. Leaves have three prominent veins.

Lower right: Five-veined sunflower. Stem is tall and turns at a right-angle at the top. Lower stem leaves have five prominent veins. Tallest of the sunflowers at 4 - 6 feet.

AUTUMN

AUTUMN is a special time, when the crowds of summer have thinned and the sky deepens to cobalt blue as raking sunlight ignites the golden aspen leaves. Sweet and melancholy, every day is a gift filled with beauty, as if the natural world were putting on a show of extravagant color, enough to satiate us for the coming season of black and white.

"Fall is absolutely my favorite time of year."

...just about everybody

A Brief Natural History of Fall Colors

After a summer of producing glucose to store in the roots, deciduous trees and shrubs begin to shut down. At the base of each leaf is a layer of cells called the abscission. During the summer, minute tubes pass through this layer, carrying water to the leaf, and carrying glucose back to the tree.

When fall arrives and sunlight is reduced, the abscission swells and turns corky, eventually cutting off the flow between leaf and branch. Without water from the tree, chlorophyll is no longer being made in the leaf. As the chlorophyll fades, pigments remaining in the leaves show their glory. These pigments are most concentrated after a dry summer and a typical Jackson Hole autumn of sunny days and cool nights.

The abscission slowly forms a seal between the leaf and branch. The cells that hold the leaf start to disintegrate, and eventually the leaf falls. Sometimes all of the leaves are ready to break free at once, and when a small breeze arises it brings to the earth a shower of gold. This is an excellent time to be standing underneath.

A Secret Season: NOVEMBER

November first marks the autumnal cross-quarter day, when fall is half over. In northern latitudes, the second half of each season feels much different than the first, and some cultures have long recognized eight seasons instead of four.

That model fits well in our area: by the first of November, the deciduous trees and shrubs have lost their leaves. Color in the landscape comes from naked dogwood and willow stems.

A second "in-between" season begins, though often the mud is frozen, making for easy travel. Long shadows and deep stillness prevail.

The last migrating birds make their appearance: Swainson's and Hermit Thrushes, night-flying Snow Geese and Tundra Swans. Rough-legged Hawks arrive from the Arctic and hunt the fields of the National Elk Refuge. The soft single note of the Townsend's Solitaire rings in lower Cache Creek canyon and the land rests, waiting for snow.

Low light, deep shadows, and bright contrast between pale aspen trunks, rusty willows, and the conifers beyond paint a unique late-fall palette.

PART II: THE TRAILS

Lower Cache Creek

Putt-putt

Cache Creek Sidewalk

Hagen

Ferrin's

Upper Cache Creek

A Choice of Trails

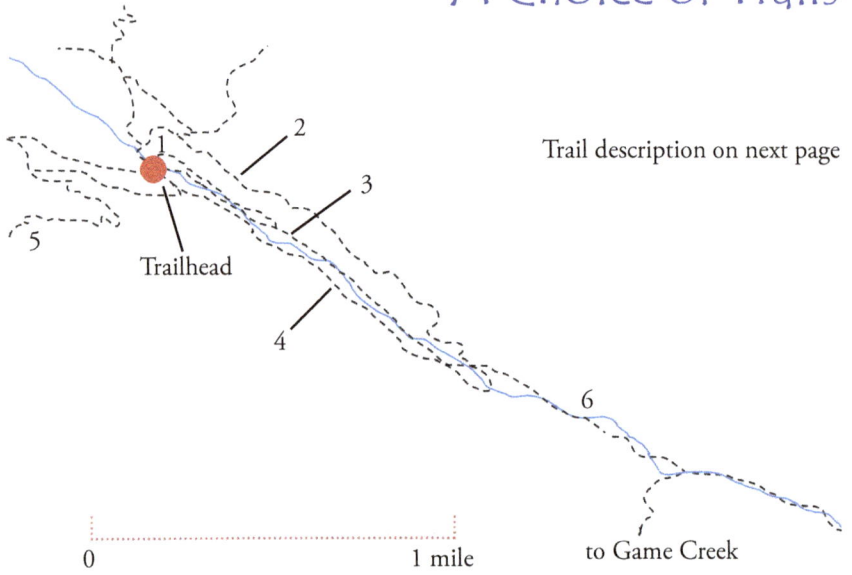

1

2

3

4

5

6

Trailhead

0   1 mile

to Game Creek

Trail description on next page

Cross-sectional view of the trails, looking east from the main trailhead.

Upper Cache Creek trails

Ferrin's Trail

Putt-putt Trail

Hagen Trail

Sidewalk Trail

Cache Creek Trail

The trails in this book are well maintained, easy to find, and display the wide diversity of natural phenomena seen in Cache Creek. Detailed trail maps are posted at the trailhead and can be obtained from the Bridger-Teton National Forest.

1. The Lower Cache Trail is the heart of the area, a trail for all seasons. About 1.7 miles long.

2. The Putt-putt Trail traverses south-facing slopes, wildlife winter range, and aspen stands. 4.7 miles long.

3. The Cache Creek Sidewalk hosts abundant wildflowers, winter sun, and a variety of mountain shrub habitats. 1.5 miles long.

4. The Hagen Trail passes through moist conifer forest and wetlands where unique plants can be found. 3 miles long.

5. Ferrin's Trail bears witness to changes with elevation and to the effects of fire and insects. Fine views on top. 2 miles from junction with Hagen Trail.

6. Upper Cache Creek abounds with wildlife and wild land. Here lies the headwaters of the creek, with places to study the area's geology, subalpine and alpine life zones, and to get a feel for true wilderness. The main trail runs for 6 miles, with several side trails in the upper end.

The Main Attraction: Cache Creek Trail

How far: 1.7 miles to a high point and wide spot in the trail (the old trailhead).

How hard: Easy going, a wide trail with gentle hills, suitable for families.

Where to start: Main Cache Creek trailhead. The trail starts at the east end where the road is gated.

What's Special: This is the place to go if you are looking for fine mountain views, access to the creek, and a chance to visit with friends or family along the way.

Dragonfly on mountain coneflower.

Cache Creek Trail Map

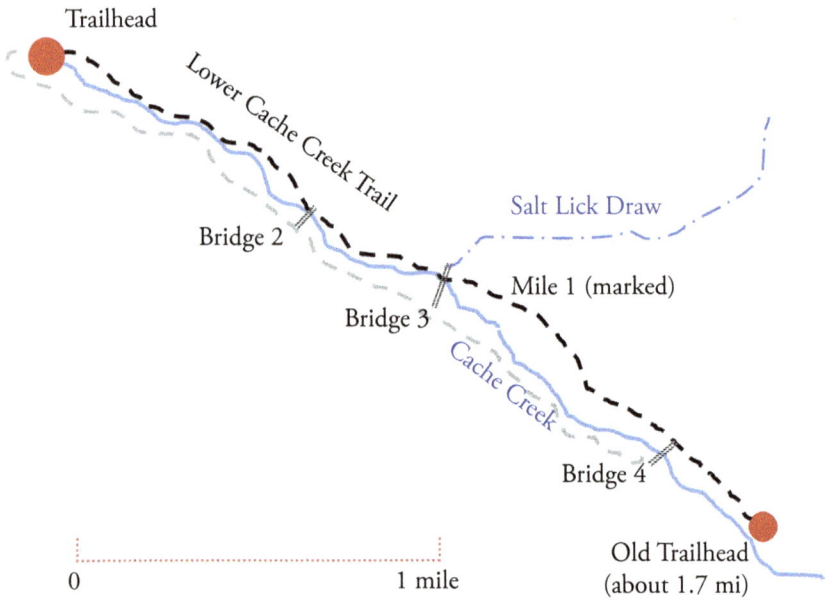

Trailhead

Lower Cache Creek Trail

Bridge 2

Salt Lick Draw

Bridge 3

Mile 1 (marked)

Cache Creek

Bridge 4

0   1 mile

Old Trailhead
(about 1.7 mi)

Nearly as famous as the Cowboy Bar, this trail is visited by dozens of people each day and about twice as many dogs. From mid-December into March, the Teton County Parks and Recreation Department grooms the trail for skiing. In summer, people on foot, bikes and horses share the trail.

There's hardly a day in the year when you can't enjoy this trail. It's the central core of a trail system with loop opportunities and five bridges crossing the creek to reach the Hagen Trail on the other side. It's the place to take company, who will remind you, with their exclamations, what it is like to see Cache Creek for the first time. It's a trail where you can feel safe from becoming lost. Since it has no real 'destination', you can turn around at any time.

Did you know? Cache Creek has over 300 species of flowering plants, including 54 species of native trees and woody shrubs.

The striking effects of aspect (the direction a slope faces) on vegetation are on display here. Sagebrush and aspen dominate the south-facing slopes in the foreground, while forest cloaks the slope opposite.

This happens in semi-dry climates like Jackson Hole where moisture needed for plant growth is in short supply. Rain or snow falls everywhere, but the south-facing slopes dry faster in the sun than more shaded north-facing aspects. Once trees are established, they shade the slopes even more, perpetuating the cooler, moister environment.

Cache Creek is an excellent place to see large stands of aspen (bright green trees at left), an important species from an ecological standpoint and one of the highlights of the trail. It spreads from root sprouts over a long period of time—a handy attribute for a tree whose seeds must land on sandy soil that stays very wet for much of the summer. Here are a few of the ways aspen contributes to the ecology of Cache Creek:

Aspens protect mountainsides and filter runoff, yielding high-quality water. The trees, along with understory plants and their litter, cover the soil, reducing surface erosion. The root systems penetrate and anchor the soil.

The stands often colonize unstable slopes, providing the best natural protection possible in places subject to landslides and slumps. When the slump occurs anyway, the trees go along for the ride and keep growing.

Finally, aspens provide habitat and food for a large number of birds and mammals.

A Hidden Gem: Some Seriously Large TREES

The lower main trail includes a spruce bottom dominated by old Engelmann spruce and a hybrid between Engelmann and Colorado spruce, as these species readily combine. Some of the trees are 15 feet around and 5 feet in diameter.

Many are dying from a combination of insects, disease, and plain old age. As the older trees die and fall over they open the forest floor to a succession of deciduous shrubs that need sunlight. The spruce trunks take years to decay, but they will eventually serve as nurse logs for those seeds that fall within reach of the nutrients they release.

The waning generation of old spruce trees forms the foundation for a new forest as shade-tolerant seedlings begin to grow under the protection of the deciduous shrubs. In the meanwhile, it's a pleasure to pause beneath one of the old matriarchs of the spruce bottom, and contemplate all the seasons she has weathered in her long life.

UNEXPECTED WONDERS: Cache Creek is full of delightful surprises. A fall storm lifts to reveal snow-covered peaks (left). A sagebrush moth appears from afternoon shadows and lights beside the trail (above).

The Putt-putt Trail

How far: 4.7 miles including the section beginning at Nelson Circle trailhead.

How hard: Moderate. The trail climbs and drops over spur ridges, with level sections in between.

Where to start: The trail can be accessed from the main Cache Creek trailhead and Nelson Drive. Signs at trail junctions direct you to the Putt-putt and other trails that lead from it.

What's Special: Views across the valley to the southern Tetons, splendid wildflower displays, fall colors, ridges for views and wooded valleys for shade.

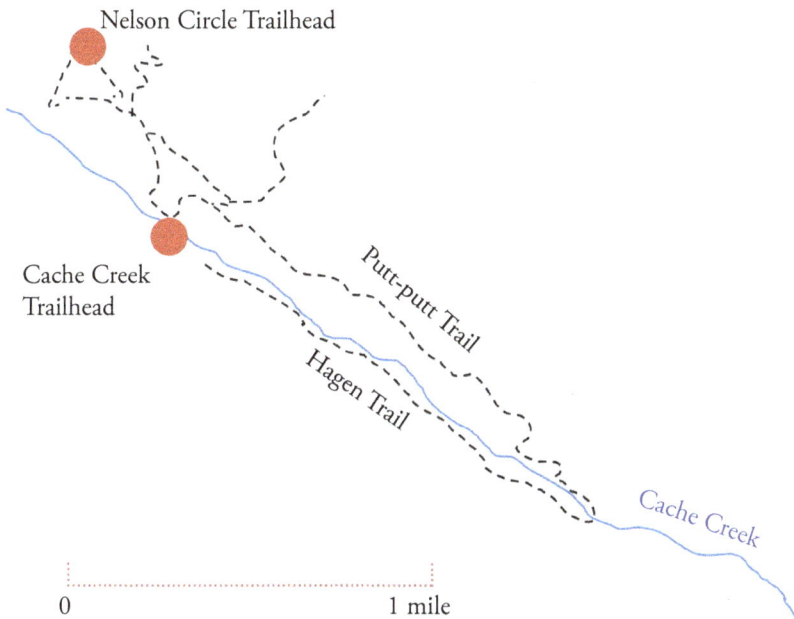

Sketch map of the Putt-putt Trail, showing its length in both directions from the main trailhead and a secondary access point at Nelson Circle.

Named for its origins as a motorbike route, this trail has been rede-signed and reconstructed over the years to serve bikers, hikers, and trail runners. In winter, the trail passes through critical winter range for elk, mule deer, and moose, and these animals are often seen near the western end of the trail.

From the edge of Jackson to the far end of the trail over two miles away, the Putt-putt offers a ramble through a variety of plant communi-ties, with wildflowers at your feet and several loops with other trails. On the west side of the trail are two junctions where the Putt-putt connects with the Crystal Butte and Woods Canyon trails, either of which will get you up high in a hurry.

Fine views, a multitude of showy wildflowers, and large stands of aspen are among the sweet features of the Putt-putt Trail. A closer look reveals the more subtle ecological nuances along the way.

These slopes are very dry. Winter's snow doesn't last long and exposure to winter winds keeps vegetation sparse. Uphill from the trail, nearly vertical tilted limestone beds crop out, forming structural protection, traces of moisture, and microclimates where trees and hardy shrubs can get a foothold.

Patches of Douglas-fir, Rocky Mountain juniper and curl-leaf ma-hogany have gotten their start where the limestone reflects the sun's warmth, its porousness captures water, and its crevices offer shelter for tender seedlings.

Browse plants are available for deer and moose (antelope bitterbrush, serviceberry, and curl-leaf mahogany are some favorites), while exposed grasses are reachable by elk. Other shrubs include spineless horsebrush, chokecherry (left), spreading juniper, two species of rabbitbrush and three species of sagebrush.

The combination of shelter and browse, accessible grasses, and a chance to retreat upslope from the frigid valley-bottom air that collects during temperature inversions makes this ideal big game winter range. The winter ranges are closed to public entry from December 1 through April 30 to minimize disturbance to wildlife.

Right: Mule deer buck on winter range.

Left: Cones ("berries") of Rocky Mountain juniper, favored by Townsend's Solitaires, Bohemian Waxwings, American Robins, and other wintering birds.

Lower Putt-putt / Woods Canyon highlights

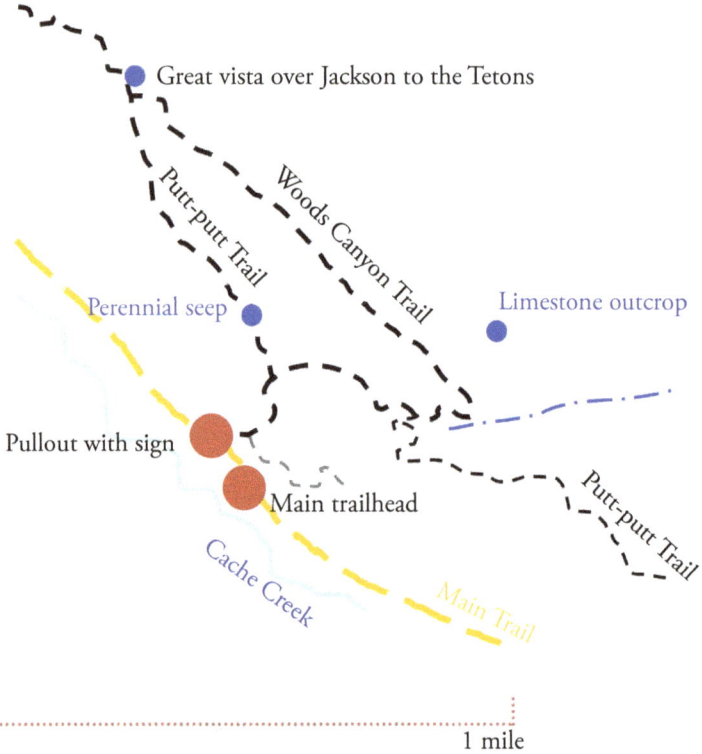

Great vista over Jackson to the Tetons

Putt-putt Trail

Woods Canyon Trail

Perennial seep

Limestone outcrop

Pullout with sign

Main trailhead

Putt-putt Trail

Cache Creek

Main Trail

0   1 mile

Oregon grape.

From the "upper" (top of the hill) parking area in Cache Creek, the trail leads north over a sagebrush-covered rise and into a lovely aspen stand. In May, watch for sagebrush buttercups, sugarbowls, shooting stars and spring beauty along the trail. Climb gentle switchbacks to the fork in the trail where the loop begins. The following description is for a clockwise circumnavigation, so you will take a left turn at the trail junction.

The trail follows the southern front of the Gros Ventre Range, where sunlight hits the ground with more intensity than it does in the draws. The kinds of plants found in the open thrive in the drier environment. Oregon grape (facing page) is one of the first plants to bloom, with brilliant yellow clusters of flowers that attract bees and send their scent along the trail. It has waxy, leathery leaves that protect the plant from the drying effects of the sun.

Another early bloomer along the trail is the magnificent arrowleaf balsamroot (below). Mature specimens take decades to grow, and as their clumps of silver-gray leaves increase, their thick, ropy tap roots dive deeper. The soft silver color of the leaves is caused by tiny hairs on the surface of the leaf, another adaptation to aridity. The hairs reflect the sun and capture water droplets from rain or dew.

Balsamroot sends its arrowhead-shaped leaves up from the center of the previous year's dead stems and can grow an inch per day when the weather is warm. Flower buds start to develop immediately and the first blossoms open like sunny banners along the sage-green slope, as if to trumpet the extravaganza of flowering to come.

Arrowleaf balsamroot.

By August the seeds are set, to be eaten by songbirds such as Pine Siskins and rodents. Least chipmunks will sometimes pile their bounty on flat stones to dry for winter storage. The leaves wither into paper-dry shells and the plant goes dormant until the following spring, with enough moisture and nutrients stored in its massive tap root to carry it through until the next year's tender green shoots emerge.

The trail continues to rise along the side of the mountain until reaching the intersection where the Putt-putt heads west to the Nelson Drive trailhead and the upper leg of the loop heads east to Woods Canyon.

To finish the loop, continue downhill to the junction with the Woods Canyon Trail (there is a sign). The Woods Canyon Trail follows the same slope as the Putt-putt, but at a higher level and on a gentler grade. Follow it to the east as it descends into the bottom of Woods Canyon, with views of impressive standing-on-end limestone outcrops high above the trail. Signs direct you back to where you began, along the Cache Creek Road.

A HIDDEN GEM: An unexpectedly glorious view of town and the Tetons. A grassy high point before the trail descends to the west is a great spot for views of Jackson, High School and Saddle Buttes, Teton Pass and the Snake River Range beyond.

FOR THE ADVENTUROUS

The Putt-putt offers some opportunities for loops with other trails. It connects with the Crystal Butte and Woods Canyon trails near the western end, the two trails close to town that quickly gain elevation.

The Crystal Butte Trail is very steep, with loose gravel in places, as its switchbacks ascend the mountain front. The views are well worth the effort. You can see the Snake River Range, the Salt Rivers beyond, and the northern peaks of the Wyoming Range, as well as the southern Tetons.

You don't have to reach the top of the trail to experience the expansive views or wildflowers that grace the trailside in May and June. Brilliant red and orange paintbrush (below) is one of the showiest; it is joined by arrowleaf balsamroot, stemless goldenweed, and blue flax. Shaggy old Douglas-firs and limber pines offer shade above the open grasslands.

Cache Creek Sidewalk Trail

How far: 1.5 miles.

How hard: Easy. The trail follows the slope not far from the main Cache Creek Trail.

Where to start: The trail can be accessed from the main Cache Creek trailhead at two locations: one next to the closed gate at the start of the Cache Creek Trail, the other next to an informal parking spot just west of the main trailhead. Signs along the start of the trail will direct you.

What's Special: A great place for early wildflowers in May as well as the tallest of the sunflower family in July; a large aspen stand, and sunshine in winter.

Helianthella and geranium.

Sidewalk Trail highlights

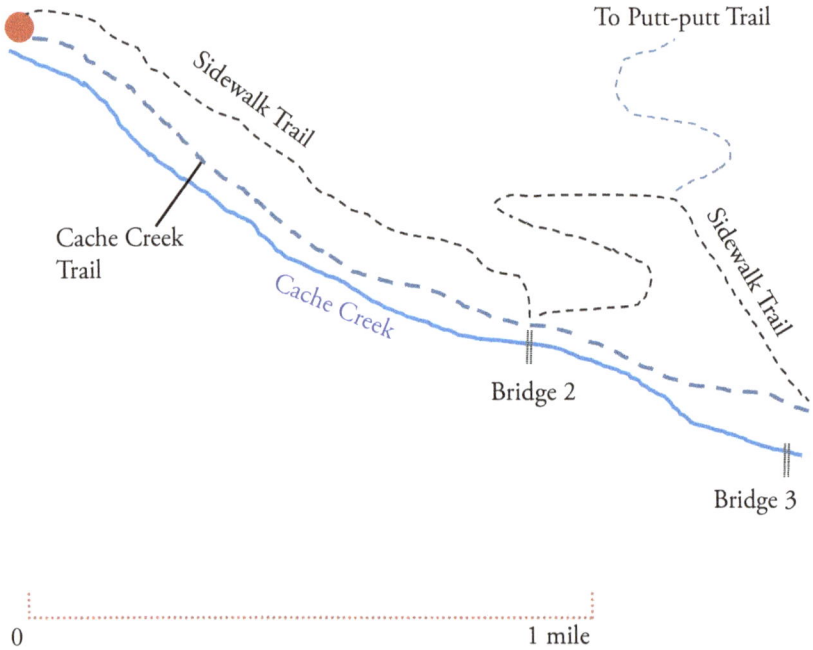

Serviceberry. Note the dense clusters of blooms with long petals and obvious teeth on the margins of the leaves. Leaves are prominently veined. Serviceberry blooms in late May.

Built to reduce congestion in lower Cache Creek, the Sidewalk Trail has been extended to traverse about a mile up the canyon. The first trail to melt out in spring, it's a good place to catch early flowers. This trail is a recommended wander on a dark winter day as well. While the creek lies in deep shadow, you can find sun on the Sidewalk for a couple of hours in mid-day. Views across the valley to Rendezvous Mountain help brighten the scene when you think spring might have forgotten to come.

When spring does appear, this trail is a delight of wildflowers and lime-green leaves. Flowers hem the trailside all summer and fall colors light the way like amber lanterns until snow falls once again.

The mountain shrub community is well represented along the Cache Creek Sidewalk. Chokecherry and serviceberry offer springtime blooms and patches of shade on the otherwise exposed slope. Similar in size and habit, these two shrubs often grow together.

Attracted to the diverse deciduous tree and shrub habitat, butterflies and songbirds abound. Black-headed Grosbeaks, Cassin's Finches, Western Tanagers and Broad-tailed Hummingbirds are among the beautiful birds along this short but delightful trail.

Chokecherry. Flowers are borne on long panicles and each flower is smaller and more compact than serviceberry. The leaves are long, pointed and leathery, with a definite shine. Teeth along the leaf margins are minute. Bloom time is usually early June.

The Sidewalk has some of the earliest
wildflowers…

Clockwise from upper left: Hood's phlox, Indian potato, shooting star, Jove's (or Utah) buttercup, and steer's head.

Whether cup- or funnel-shaped, symmetrical or oddly lobed, wildflowers are all designed for the same thing: pollination. The yellow violet (right) has contrasting dark streaks that point toward the center of the flower, guiding insects to its cache of pollen and nectar.

The insect enters the flower to harvest nectar and doing so, brushes against the anthers. Pollen sticks to its back and wings, and the next flower it visits receives a bit of the pollen. By visiting different plants, the insect facilitates the development of fertile seeds.

We think of bees and butterflies as pollinators, but a variety of other insects can do the job. Many pollinate specific plant genera that depend on them, and, like the orange-tip butterfly at left, select a specific type of plant to lay eggs on. The orange-tip uses rockcress as its host (as well as for nectaring, as seen here).

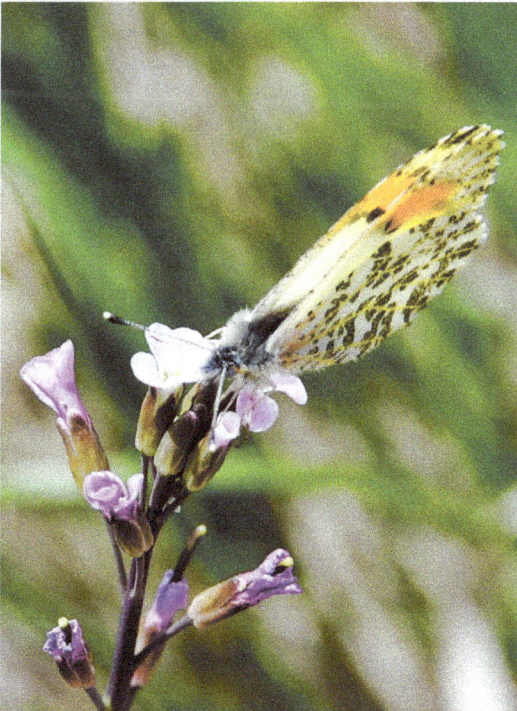

Some plants let the wind take care of pollination. Most of these have inconspicuous blooms and little scent since they don't need to attract a bug. Conifers and aspens are wind-pollinated plants.

Speaking of flowers…

Adding to the sunshine of an open slope is a variety of bright-yellow flowers from the diminutive buttercup to saw groundsel and five-veined sunflower, which can exceed six feet. Here's a list of yellow flowers in roughly the order of bloom.

Long-stalk spring-parsley
Nineleaf biscuitroot
Fernleaf biscuitroot
Oregon grape
Wallflower
3 species of yellow violet
Western groundsel
Nodding microseris
Arrowleaf balsamroot
Western yellow paintbrush
Sharpleaf hawk's beard
Hound's-tongue hawkweed
Antelope bitterbrush
Slender cinquefoil
White cinquefoil
Little sunflower
Five-veined sunflower
Saw groundsel
Goldenrod
Spineless horsebrush
Rubber rabbitbrush
Green rabbitbrush
Western sagewort
Showy goldeneye
Mountain big sage

Goldenrod and yampah.

If you're angry, blue, or just plain frazzled, this is the place for you—nature's abundance can't help but bring a smile.

Blue copper visiting a sulfur flower.

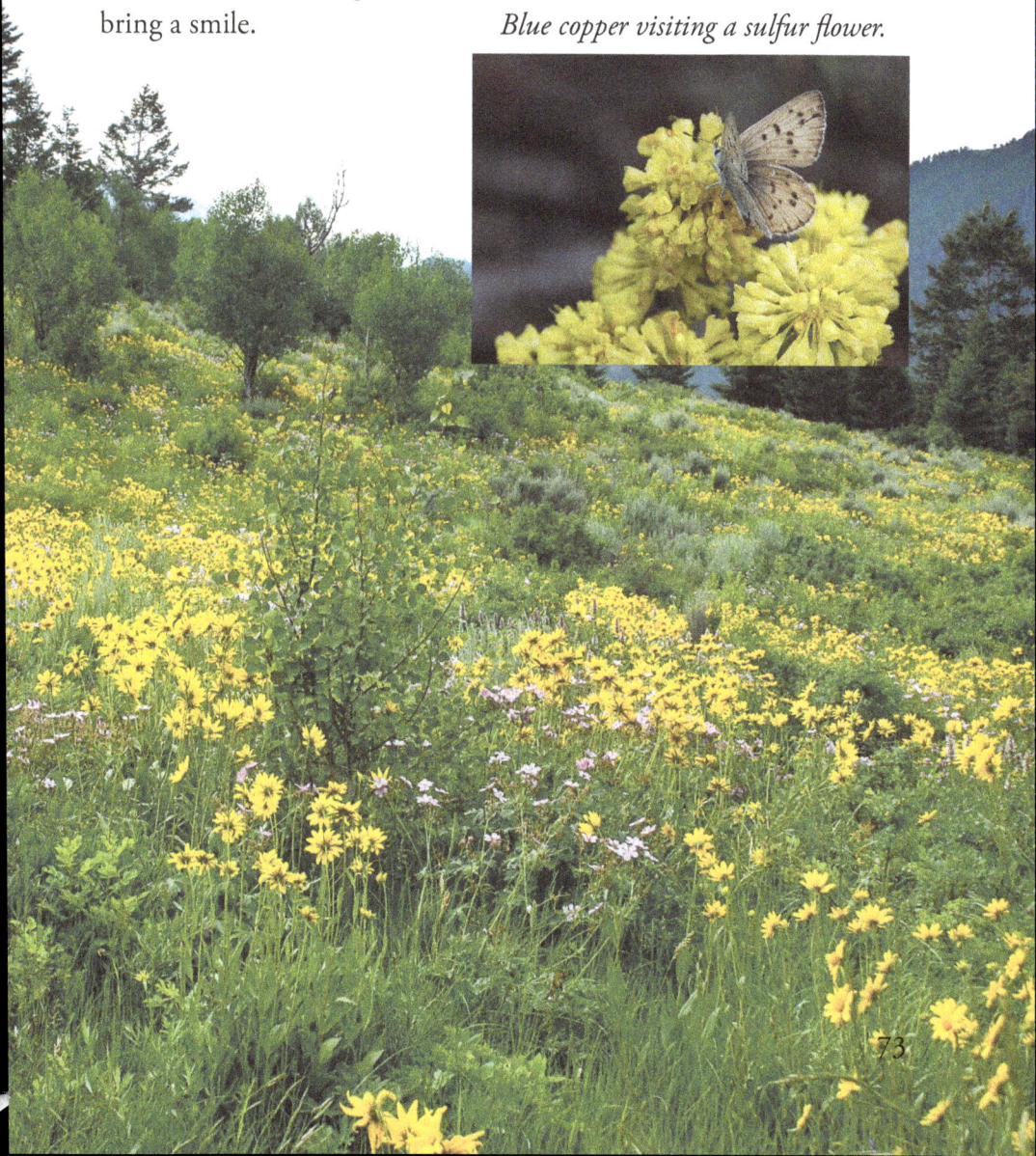

A bloom of a different color...

Crucifer rust on rockcress.

If you have ever been fooled by this early splash of yellow, you're not alone. It's designed to trick pollinators. What is going on?

The "pseudoflowers" pictured here on a rockcress are made by a fungus called crucifer rust (it is specific to members of the mustard family or Cruciferae). It invades the upper leaves and turns them into bright yellow roses covered with sweet, sticky nectar.

Along with nectar are fungal reproductive cells called spermatia. Insects transfer male and female spermatia to other pseudo-flowers, thus enabling sexual reproduction of the rust.

What's in it for the rockcress? Infected plants host the fungus for the rest of the growing season and it prevents them from creating their own blooms. But not every plant is hit, so it's possible that the bright yellow pseudoflowers, larger and more conspicuous than the rockcress' own small white blooms, attract more pollinators to the general area. Flowering plants as a group benefit.

Mature rust spores.

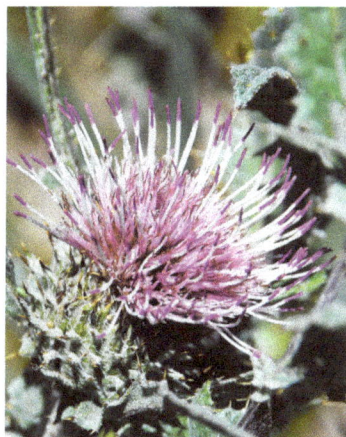

The Prickly Ones

Tall and shaggy and covered with thorns, thistles are distinctive among the plants along the Sidewalk Trail. People often dismiss them as unpleasant weeds. But two of the thistles pictured here are native plants.

Elk thistle (above left) is found on the upper Sidewalk and other trails. It has a dense cluster of flowers and leaves on top of a single stem. Typically 3 feet tall, it is often found in shade. Elk and horses relish the artichoke-like flowers.

Like elk thistle, Teton thistle (upper right), is native to the local area, thus its name. Its hairy foliage and long yellow thorns on the leaf margins help identify it. Its upper main stem has branches.

The non-native musk thistle (below right) grows to 6 or more feet. With large flower heads full of seeds, it can become dominant if allowed to take over, and like many non-native weeds, it detracts from the quality of native habitat and biodiversity. Bees and butterflies, of course, love thistles of any kind.

A goshawk hunts while his mate incubates the eggs.

The Hagen Trail

How far: 3 miles one way. Bridges crossing Cache Creek offer loop opportunities.

How hard: Moderate. The trail climbs in a few places but mostly follows gentle terrain. Shade of the forest makes this a good choice for a hot summer day.

Where to start: The main Cache Creek trailhead. Cross at the first bridge just west of the parking area.

What's Special: Forest shade, wildflowers not seen elsewhere, riparian area and access to the creek.

Bridge 1

Trailhead

Cache Creek

Hagen Trail

Bridge 2

Bridge 3

0

1 mile

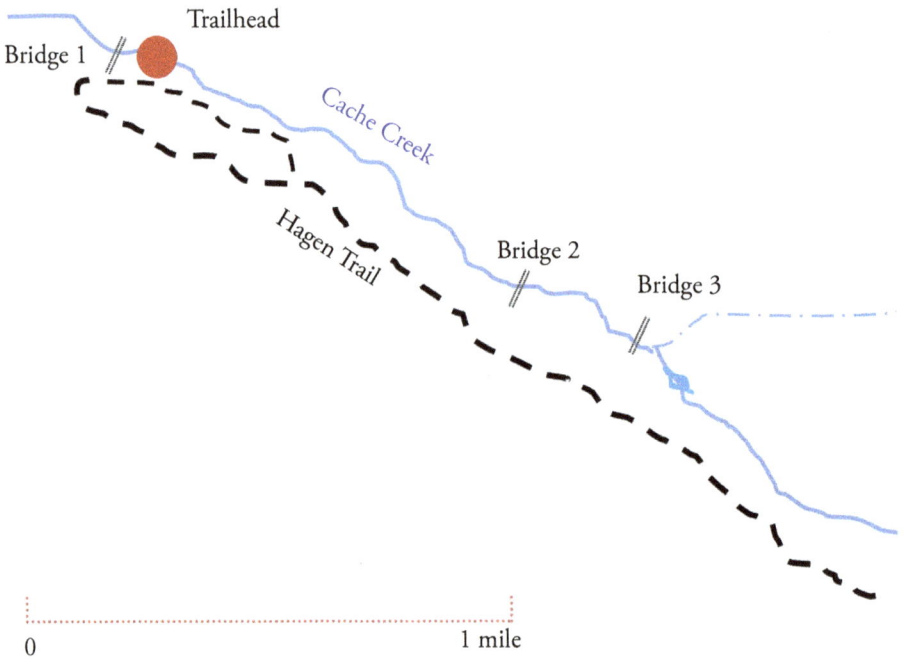

Hagen Trail highlights

Wild strawberry is found in abundance along the Hagen Trail.

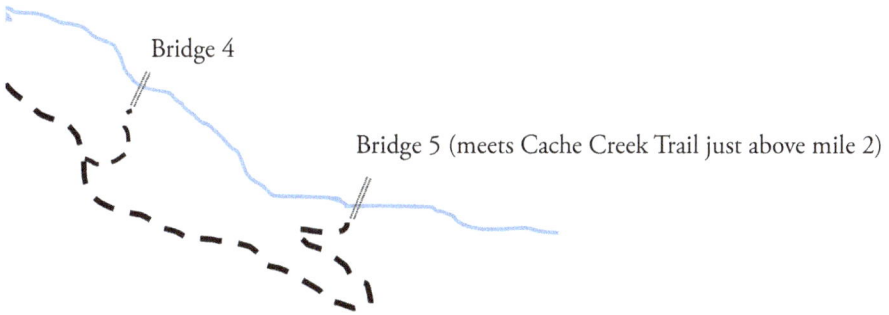

Bridge 4

Bridge 5 (meets Cache Creek Trail just above mile 2)

On the shady side of Cache Creek, this trail passes through cool moist terrain with enough openings to add views and variety. Accessible from the main trail via five bridges along its length, the Hagen is the best trail to see forest-dwelling plants and animals, as well as wetland species not found elsewhere.

Western clematis, one of the few native vines in the area.

Fairy slipper, an orchid seen in few places other than the Hagen Trail.

Twinflower, a dainty ground cover, seen only near the upper end of the Hagen Trail.

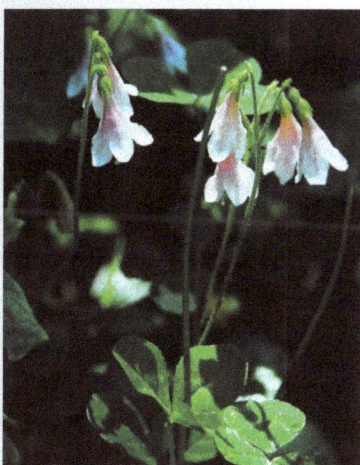

Did you know? The trail is named for Grant O. ('Tiny') Hagen, a well-known local artist. His drawings adorn Frank and John Craighead's *Field Guide to Rocky Mountain Wildflowers*.

The Hagen Trail invites attention to detail. Those who accept the invitation are rewarded with delightful discoveries. The wildflowers on these pages are examples of those found along this trail but not seen often—or at all—elsewhere in Cache Creek.

Lewis' monkeyflower.

Twisted stalk.

Wood nymph.

Baneberry.

Fairy bell (flower).

Fairy bell (fruit).

Five-stamen miterwort.

Meadow rue.

Living fossils

Scouring rush, which resembles a three-foot forest of slim green pipes, and the lacy foot-tall field horsetail, are survivors. Ancestral horsetails once grew with giant tree ferns and cycads in the tropical climates of Devonian times (close to 400 million years ago). They lived and died for many millions of years, and once buried and compressed, became the rock we now call coal. Their diminutive progeny thrive today.

Horsetails store nutrients in their stems, which are delivered to the surface of the soil when the stems die. Other plants that benefit from horsetail nutrient pumping are sedges and deciduous shrubs.

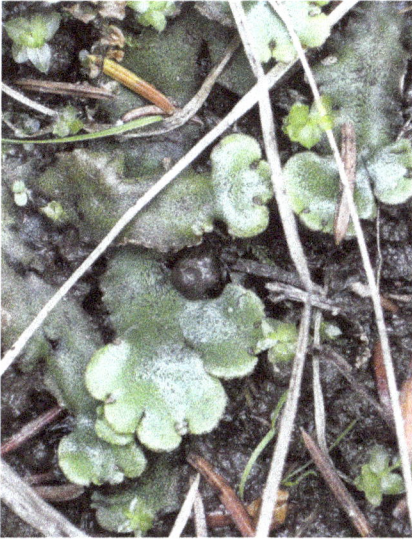

Other ancient plants that thrive near the Hagen Trail include mosses, bryophytes, and liverwort (left), the most visible of which are flat, ground-hugging thallose forms that grow in spreading colonies. They are among the oldest land plants on earth, even more ancient than horsetails. Fossil liverwort spores have been found in Middle Ordovician strata, dating from around 470 million years ago.

Look for these plants where it is damp and shady, usually near the creek. There is a nice cluster of them below bridge 4.

While you're peering into the muck, you may be surprised to see some other lovely denizens of the forest floor, fungi.

Fungus takes many forms, but one of the most familiar is the mushroom. These puffballs are growing on a rotten log, but with the nest of moss surrounding them, they resemble eggs.

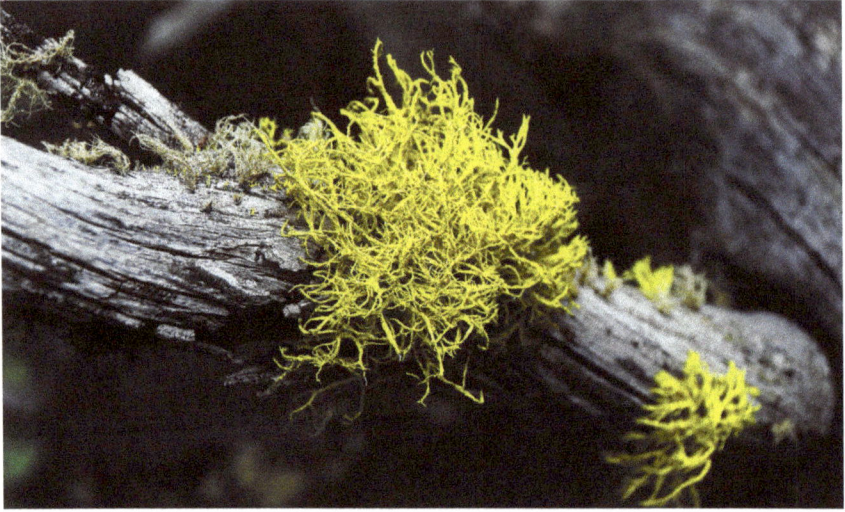

Above: Wolf lichen on the branch of a fallen log.

Fossils also attest to the longest marriage on earth, between algae and fungi. We know this union as lichen, and there is plenty of it to be seen along the Hagen Trail. The primary forms of lichen here are foliose (leaf-like), crustose (dense and small, like the kind found on rocks), and fruticose (branching, resembling hair or miniature trees). Lichens are sensitive to pollutants, so their presence means clean air.

Right: Ground-dwelling foliose lichen.

Lichens are useful: they fix atmospheric nitrogen for use by plants, and are eaten by flying squirrels and red-backed voles. They provide fresh greens for cervids (deer, elk, moose) whose winter diets would otherwise consist of dead grass and dormant twigs.

Birds and small mammals use lichens to line their nests. People use lichens for medicine and as a source of natural dye. Wolf lichen, common in the forest here, turns wool a lovely bright green (dyed homespun yarn, right) that is colorfast and exudes a rich forest scent long after emerging from the dye pot.

Lichens seem to inspire whimsy in humans. Even stoic scientists get into the act, as the common names of lichen genera in the greater Yellowstone region attest:

Cobblestone	Vinyl
Tree-hair	Rock-posy
Pixie cup	Rock tripe
Trumpet	Old man's beard
Tarpaper	Sunshine
Jellyskin	Yellow ruffle

Pixie cups (Cladonia sp.) on a stump.

Something New

An evolving sight along the Hagen Trail is a series of beaver ponds just upstream from Bridge 3. This willow bottom along Cache Creek had been without evident beaver activity for years, until 2013, when new arrivals began construction. The beavers are most likely related to those whose pond can be seen on private land just below the forest boundary. Both pond complexes are expanding.

Water seeps among the dams into low spots among the willows where sedges and other aquatic plants grow. This creates habitat for waterfowl, fish, aquatic invertebrates, and amphibians such as boreal chorus frogs, whose peeping can be heard in early May.

A few years later, nesting mallards and gadwalls have found the new ponds. Fish have found them. Ospreys have found the fish. Stay tuned for more changes to come.

Left: Comma butterfly on aster.
Right: Flower spider in ambush mode on lupine. (Not hiding very well!)

Find a sunny opening along the trail and beside the creek, and you are sure to find a cluster of butterflies. If they happen to fly when you approach, you may see that they have been sitting on a pile of doggie doo (as the fritillaries and blues pictured here are doing).

It's startling to watch these lovely insects belly up to the dung bar, but for them it is all about obtaining necessary nutrients. They taste

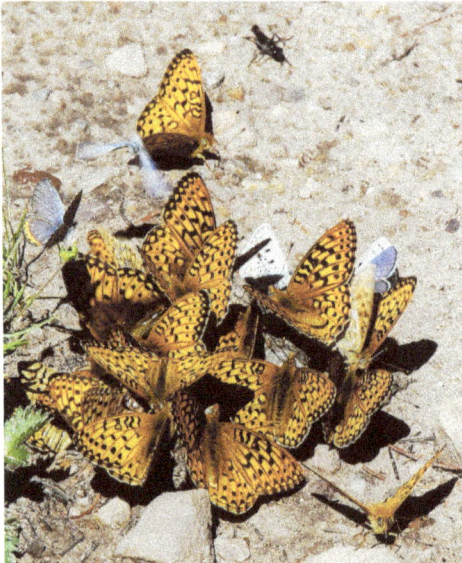

through organs in their feet called tarsi, while their antennae detect scents. When these organs register the presence of nutrients, they unfurl their coiled prosboci and feed.

In early spring there are few flowers to offer nectar, so scat provides a welcome snack. Mud beside the creek is likewise full of minerals and dissolved organic particles the butterflies need.

Wildlife in the Woods

It's not all about deer and elk in these parts. Most of the larger wildlife move around at night when people aren't there to disturb them. You will likely see tracks and "sign" (scat) that show who has passed along the trail, but most of the wildlife you will encounter are small creatures. Here are a few of them.

Not often seen during the day, the pine marten (lower right) is a predator subsisting primarily on red squirrels and other small rodents. The Hagen Trail, with its mixed old growth forest, makes ideal habitat for this intelligent, curious, and agile species. Red squirrels (lower left) have learned to make them-selves invisible when standing still in a pine tree. The ruffed grouse (upper right) can be found on nearly all the trails in Cache Creek.

Ferrin's Trail

How far: 2 miles from the junction with the Upper Hagen Trail.

How hard: Strenuous. The trail climbs 1200 feet from the trailhead to the top of the divide with Wilson Canyon.

Where to start: The trail can be accessed from the Upper Hagen Trail (see map on next page). Park at the main Cache Creek trailhead and follow the Hagen Trail or Hagen Highway. Signs at trail junctions direct you to the Ferrin's.

What's Special: This trail climbs to the divide between Cache Creek and Wilson Canyon, where one can enjoy glorious views. It's shady on a hot day, and you will find understory flowers not seen in such profusion elsewhere in Cache Creek, including vining clematis and a variety of orchids.

Left: Ferrin's Trail winds its way through the forest.

Right: A first glimpse of the Grand from an opening in the trees.

How to reach the Ferrin's Trail

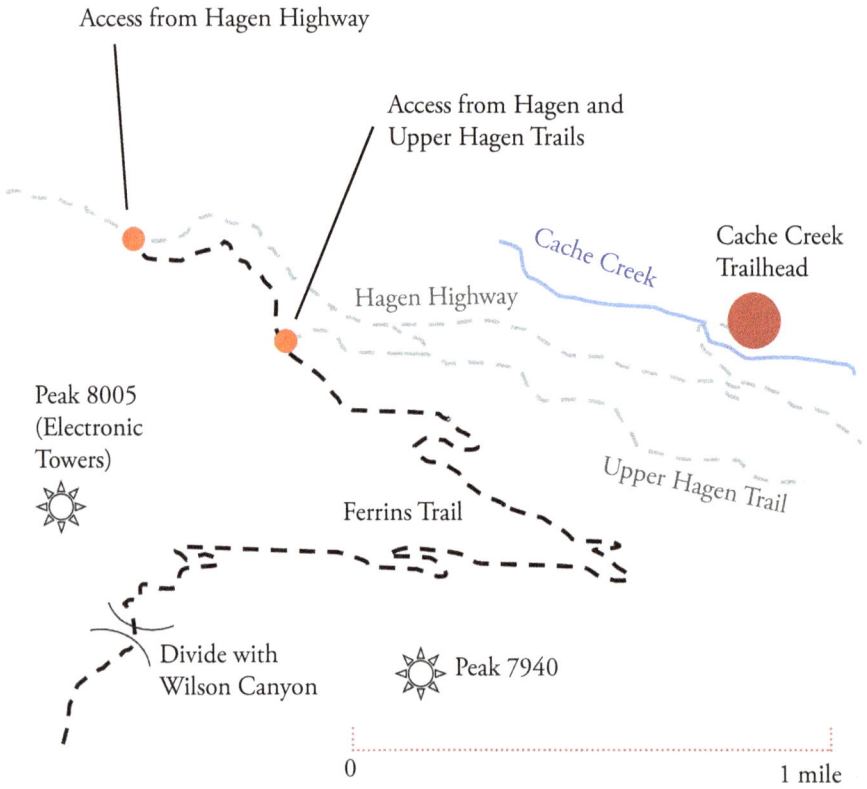

Access from Hagen Highway

Access from Hagen and
Upper Hagen Trails

Cache Creek

Cache Creek
Trailhead

Hagen Highway

Peak 8005
(Electronic
Towers)

Upper Hagen Trail

Ferrins Trail

Divide with
Wilson Canyon

Peak 7940

0   1 mile

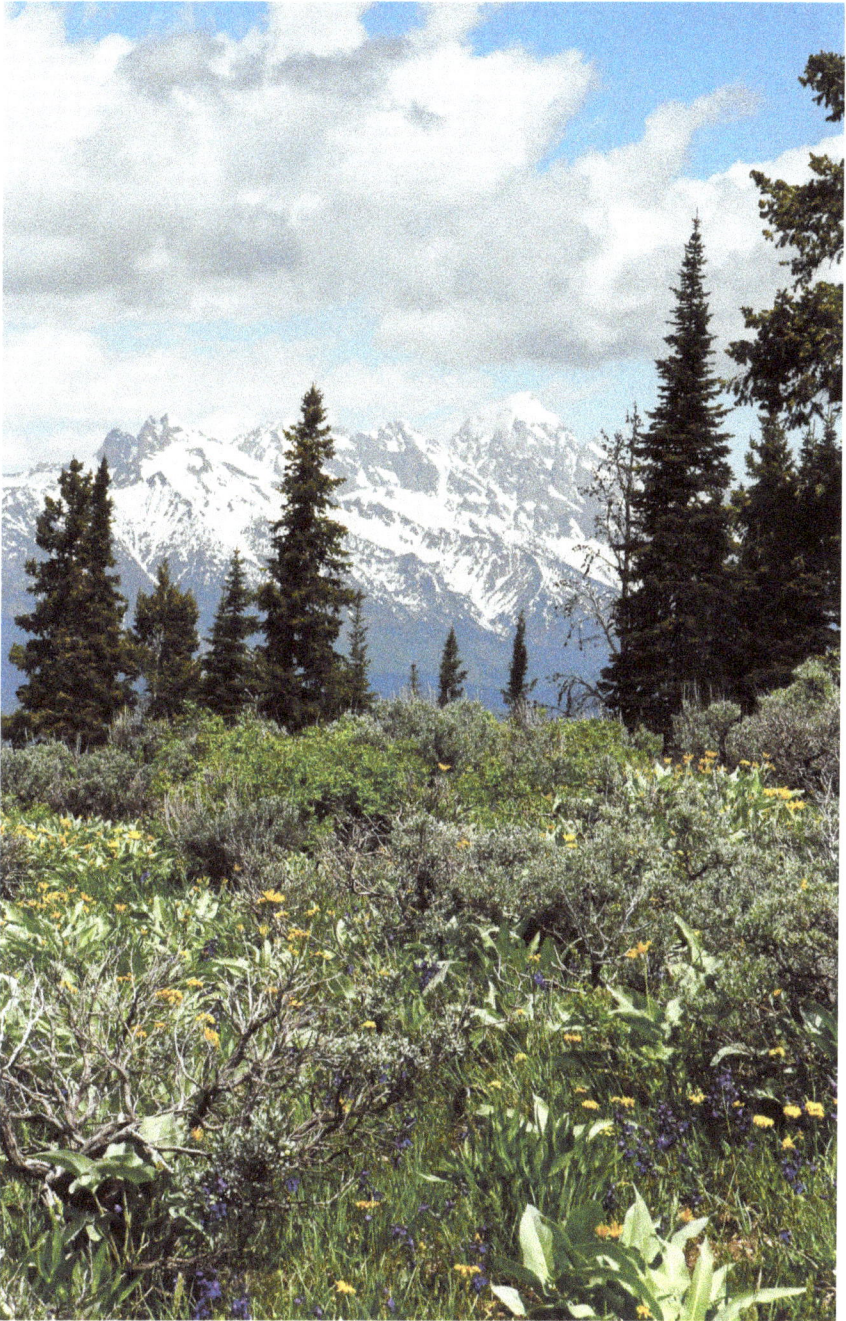

Reward for the long climb: a view of the Tetons.

Heartleaf arnica.

This trail was constructed to replace a steep route on Ferrin's Slide, where more than one avalanche has taken trees and skiers on a most unpleasant ride.

Stands of old growth forest grace the lower part of the trail. The trees are widely spaced, allowing light to penetrate to the forest floor.

A variety of wildflowers not seen in such abundance elsewhere in Cache Creek includes Colorado columbine and heartleaf arnica, shown here.

As the trail climbs the forest changes from the open park-like stands near the bottom to what foresters call dog hair—crowded, small-diameter trees that don't let much sun reach the forest floor.

This results in fewer wildflowers and more shade-tolerant ground covers, including racemose pussytoes, orchids, and side-bells pyrola.

Colorado columbine.

Understory plants include sidebells pyrola, three members of the heath family (whortleberry, pippssisewa, and pinedrops), and those orchids that do not need the perennial moisture of bogs. Fairy slipper, striped and spotted coralroot, Alaska rein orchid and rattlesnake plantain are found in patches along the trail, and each year they may crop up in a different spot.

Alaska rein orchid.

Sidebells pyrola.

Pinedrops.

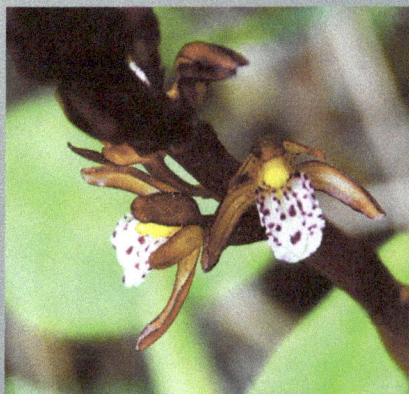
Spotted coralroot detail.

Inconspicuous unless in bloom, orchids occur along the length of the trail. Look for striped coralroot near the junction with the Upper Hagen Trail, and a nice group of rattlesnake plantain near the edge of forest before the trail breaks into the open at the top.

Rattlesnake plantain rosette of basal leaves.

Striped coralroot.

Rattlesnake plantain flowers.

99

Insects LOVE trees!

Insects are major agents of change in the conifer forest, where they eat everything from the tips of young needles (Douglas-fir damaged by budworms, upper left) to the dead wood of an old log (upper right).

Longhorn beetles, not to be confused with the mountain pine beetle, are caught in late summer making new ones (lower left). The larva of a mountain pine beetle (below right) will develop into an adult smaller than a pinkie fingernail.

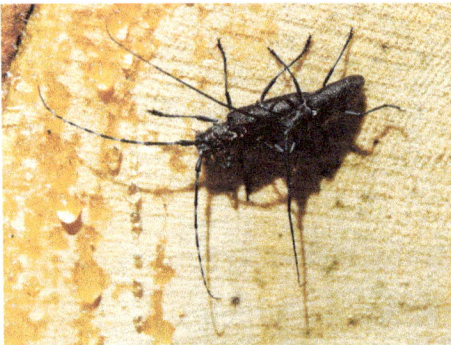

Right: "Dog hair" on the upper Ferrin's Trail. This forest was regenerated by wildfire in 1897. This dense small-diameter stand will continue to grow as it is until the next fire, windstorm, or bug infestation clears some trees away.

Below: a typical insect gall on a Douglas-fir twig. Adults lay their eggs on the tree and the grubs feed on nutrients delivered by the cambium. The gall protects the growing larvae, though clever sharp-billed birds can drill holes in it. The tiny predators of huge trees have predators of their own.

From the north side of Cache Creek, opposite the Ferrin's Trail, you can look across and see the signature of old fires, a classic 'mosaic' pattern of even-aged trees with patches of taller, shaggier specimens in between. The younger ones replaced those that burned over a century ago; the older trees remaining are those that were once young and vigorous and thus survived the fire.

In much of the greater Yellowstone region, the fire cycle in subalpine fir-spruce-lodgepole pine forests is up to two hundred years due to the high elevation and generally cool, moist conditions. Douglas-fir grows in lower and drier sites, so it burns more often. As evidenced by the 2012 Little Horsethief Fire, which burned to the margins of the Cache Creek watershed, we can be assured that this forest will burn again, as it must.

Large trees with heavy bark can often survive a fire if it doesn't reach the crowns. Ground fires clear out the understory, leaving scars on trunks of the old trees. Many fire scars like the one pictured here can be found along the Ferrin's Trail.

Large stand-replacing wildfires are typical in this region. The mosaic pattern seen on the slope east of the Ferrin's Trail (opposite page) gives ample evidence that large fires are the kind that have historically burned.

The classic fire-created mosaic

Older Douglas-fir on the sky-line, much of it now dying of old age and disease.

A patch of recently insect-killed trees.

Younger stand of Douglas-fir, started after the 1897 forest fire.

Foreground: Old spruce stand in moist valley bottom, with a longer fire cycle than that of the Douglas-fir on the slope.

Tiny, distant Snow King Mountain seen from below the Horse Creek Divide.

Upper Cache Creek Trails

How FAR: From the end of the Lower Cache Creek Trail (1.7 miles from trailhead) this trail continues another 4 miles before splitting into various directions into the Gros Ventre Wilderness.

How HARD: Easy going with gentle hills and level areas along the side of the creek.

WHERE TO START: Main Cache Creek trailhead.

WHAT'S SPECIAL: Upper trails, with the exception of the Cache-Game Creek connector, enter the Gros Ventre Wilderness. Upper Cache Creek gives access to some of the highest mountains near town, and it is the western end of the Granite Highline Trail, a 24-mile route originating near Granite Hot Springs.

Upper Cache Creek trails

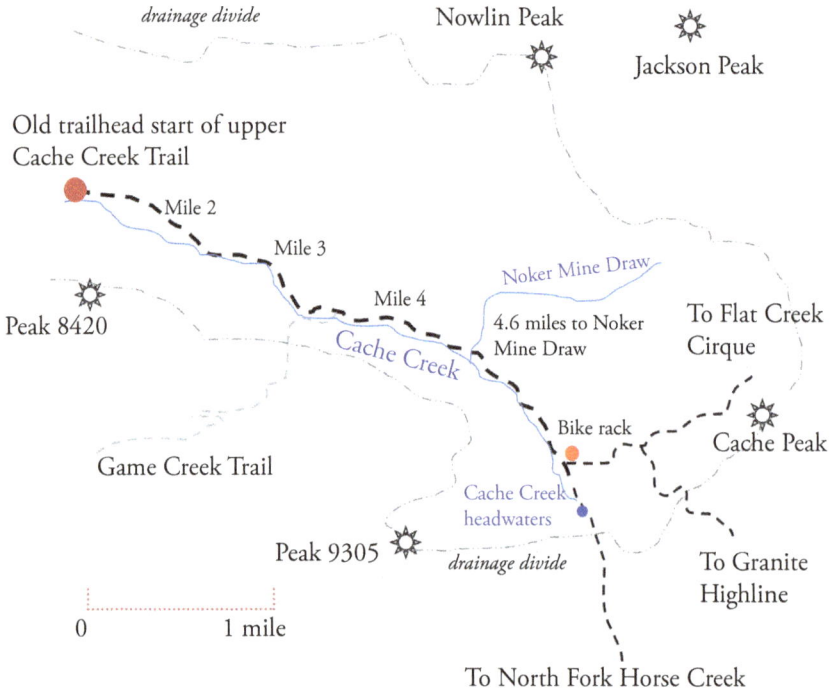

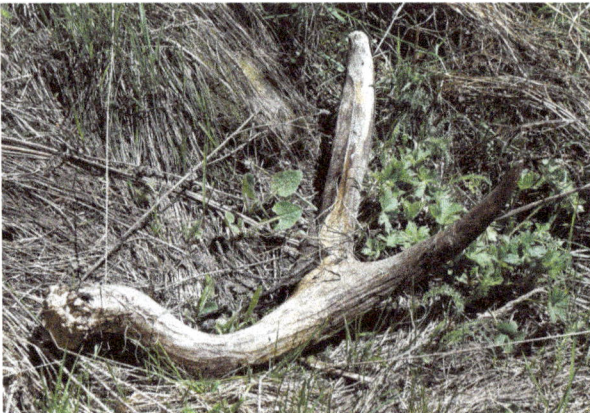

drainage divide

Nowlin Peak

Jackson Peak

Old trailhead start of upper
Cache Creek Trail

Mile 2

Mile 3

Mile 4

Noker Mine Draw

Peak 8420

Cache Creek

4.6 miles to Noker
Mine Draw

To Flat Creek
Cirque

Bike rack

Cache Peak

Game Creek Trail

Cache Creek
headwaters

Peak 9305

drainage divide

To Granite
Highline

0   1 mile

To North Fork Horse Creek

*A shed antler
chewed by rodents.*

Cascade near Game Creek cutoff.

Yellow bells.

Upper Cache Creek lies within the 318,000-acre Gros Ventre Wilderness, designated in part for its outstanding summer range for the Jackson Hole elk herd and habitat for other wildlife. The area is also recognized for its variety of geologic phenomena, from colorful cliffs to large landslides. The Gros Ventre Range has the highest concentration of landslides recorded for any mountain range in the country.

As you enter the mountain realm of upper Cache Creek you can feel the difference in character from what lies closer to town. The main trail narrows, and the native clay-soil surface holds snow and moisture well into spring. Enclosed gorge sections alternate with wide meadows and the occasional tantalizing view to the peaks ahead.

The forest is changing too, with elevation and increased moisture. Subalpine fir, spruce and lodgepole pine mix with Douglas-fir. Perennial side streams and runoff rivulets are abundant, feeding small wetlands and bogs between the trail and the creek. Near the three-mile marker you may glimpse the remains of an old road heading downslope and across the creek. This is the access to Charlie Peterson's historic outfitting camp. He led hunters into the high country for many decades from this secluded campsite.

Beyond the opening where his camp lies, the forest closes in. A refreshing cascade comes in from the north and just beyond it you'll see a fine view of Cache Peak. Watch for a stand of balsam poplar just upstream from the Game Creek cutoff trail; in this wet area you'll also find yellow

monkeyflower, white bog orchid, blue Jacob's ladder, and purple veronica.

Above: an early October snowfall etches the highest peaks. From the ridge dividing Cache and Game Creeks, one can see into the head of Cache Creek and the mountains surrounding it. The main stem of the creek angles left to right beyond the closer forested ridge. Cache Peak stands on the skyline, at the center of the photograph. Gros Peak stands high beyond Cache Creek, center right, and the divide with Horse Creek is the snowy saddle directly in front of Gros Peak.

A rushing tributary of Cache Creek tumbles across the trail at mile 5. There is no bridge, but in midsummer when the water is low, you can step across on rocks.

Beyond Noker Mine Draw (marked as Mile 4.6) the trail becomes more primitive, crossing steep clay slopes that are usually on the move, elk wallows, and patches of late snow. At about mile 5 (no markers past 4.6) the trail crosses a rushing cascade. A half-mile farther the trail splits and its branches lead deeper into the backcountry and high into the Gros Ventre Range.

Weidermeyer's admirals (left) and tiger swallowtails (above) are among the several large, showy butterflies that frequent the damp earth beside the creek.

"I believe we have a profound, fundamental need for areas of wilderness—a need that is not only recreational and spiritual, but also educational and scientific, and essential to our understanding of ourselves, our culture, our own natures, and our place in nature."
—Howard Zahniser, primary author of the 1964 Wilderness Act

Some common wildflowers of Cache Creek's high country.

Clockwise from upper left: subalpine daisy, twinpod, sky pilot, alpine sunflower and Teton cliff anemone. These are a small sample of the blooms that grace the upper slopes of Cache, Nowlin, and other nearby peaks.

Locals know this spot, though the entire Cache-Game loop is best done via bicycle if you don't want to arrange for a vehicle shuttle. One option for those seeking a long, but not too challenging hike, is to access the Game Creek cutoff trail from the Upper Cache Trail. Not far before the mile 4 marker, there is a trail junction with a sign directing you to Game Creek. Cross the bridge and follow the trail to the divide. It's not far, perhaps a half mile, to the high point. Along the way, look for scarlet and sulphur paintbrush, lupine, cinquefoil, and other wildflowers typical of a high mountain meadow.

In 4.5 miles, the elevation gain is about a thousand feet, which is a gentle stream grade for most of the distance. The bump up to the divide from the Cache Creek Trail is around 300 feet.

A Hidden Gem: The Cache-Game Divide

When you reach the top, what you will find are views down Game Creek and across upper Cache Creek to the peaks above, open meadows and conifer forest. If you travel a little ways toward Game Creek, a beautiful aspen stand surrounds the trail.

These photos were taken from the same viewpoint, a few steps up a slope from the trail.

Facing page: The view down Game Creek, which runs westward to emerge from the mountains south of Jackson.

This page: The circle of peaks wrapping the headwaters of Cache Creek. Cache Peak is the high point at the far right edge of the photo.

Part III: Cache Creek
Past, Present, and Future

Cache Creek is one of those easily accessible places that give people a feel for the larger wild land that surrounds us. In some ways Cache Creek is wilder than it was for earlier generations of Jacksonites, whose purposes it served, just as it serves ours now. Most of the roads, including old timber haul roads and jeep trails, are now hiking, horseback and biking trails. Except for the lichen-covered stumps along the Hagen trail, there is little left to see of the timbering that took place decades ago, and very little in the way of permanent structures.

Regardless of what fires and floods may bring, a lot of folks would probably like to see the area remain pretty much the way it is now. The scenery and ecology will change—either rapidly, as in the case of a large fire, or slowly, year by year. But this land is resilient, and has been responding to change for a lot longer than people have been around to watch.

Some of Jackson's oldest buildings are made of logs that came from Cache Creek.

117

If it's close to ideal the way it is, there isn't much work we have to do. Keep the weeds out, keep the water clean and clear, minimize the on-site impacts of things like trail erosion, discarded trash, and of course doggie doo. Understanding what makes this a special place is a step in maintaining our respect for it and all the places we care for.

Yet, larger threats may loom, including the pressure we place on natural resources. Some seem to believe that the public should be divested of its public land, especially in the western states. Those who disagree need to speak up. Preserving places we love requires our vigilance, for we can't afford to take anything for granted.

Did you know? A plan to build an exploratory gas well in upper Cache Creek was defeated by local citizen action in 1981.

A river once ran through it...

View of Jackson from Crystal Butte Trail.

A town wrapped in mountains: Snow King rising to the far left, the Snake River and Teton Ranges on the skyline, High School and Saddle Buttes in the middle ground. But where's Cache Creek? (Hint: imagine a diagonal line from the lower left corner of the picture to the base of Saddle Butte on the right. Pretty close to where it used to be.)

The Cache Creek watershed encompasses about 17 square miles. 37% of that total watershed is here—in town—and mostly it is underground.

Imagine a streamside parkway...

Well, why not? Other towns in the Rockies have resurrected their rivers with fabulous results. We have a fine start in Mike Yokel Park (below) on East Kelly Avenue; imagine such a parkway stretching from the confluence of Cache and Flat Creeks, through town, and into the national forest. Cache Creek could become the centerpiece of neighborhoods and the lifeblood of Jackson once more. Cache Creek is one of those places that make you want to daydream a little. In the meantime, we continue to love and enjoy those parts of it that remain.

For decades, Cache Creek was a source of raw materials for the growing town of Jackson. People hunted for their meat, cut firewood, poles, and house logs, mined coal, grazed livestock, and used the creek's water for irrigation, power and drinking. Today, Cache Creek remains important to the community: it offers rest, renewal, and recreation.

Rules and Trail Etiquette

The high level of recreation use in Cache Creek requires a few rules to keep everyone's experience a positive one. Please be aware of them.

- Trail right of way: most of the trails are open to a variety of non-motorized uses. Cyclists must yield to other trail users. Downhill cyclists yield to those going uphill. Hikers, runners and bikers yield to horses. Everyone: please display courtesy and respect for others. Slow down and share the trail.

- Dog owners: scoop the poop. Mutt-mitt stations and disposal bins are provided to help with this.

- Your dog must be under voice control (or on a leash). Dogs are not allowed to chase or otherwise harass wildlife.

- If going faster than the party ahead of you, announce your approach in advance when coming from behind. Hint: you can get bike bells for free or very low cost. Others will greatly appreciate it if you use them.

- In winter, be aware of wildlife closures and places where you need to keep your dog on a leash.

Fruit of star-flowered false Solomon-seal.

Recommended Reading

Visit any book or outdoor recreation store in Jackson and you will find a shelf of great references to the local scene from wildflower identification to trail guides. Here are a few favorites, written by experts in their fields. Take time to browse the books though—someone is always coming out with another must-have flower book.

Birds of Grand Teton National Park and the Surrounding Area, by Bert Raynes.

Butterflies of Grand Teton and Yellowstone National Parks, by Steven Poole.

Common Wildflowers of Grand Teton National Park, by Charlie Craighead and Henry Holdsworth.

Creation of the Teton Landscape, by David Love and John Reed.

Jackson Hole Hikes, by Rebecca Woods.

Local Color: Jackson Hole in Words and Watercolor, by Huntley Baldwin.

Wildflowers of Grand Teton and Yellowstone National Parks, by Richard Shaw.

Wildlife of Grand Teton National Park, by Charlie Craighead and Henry Holdsworth.

About the author

Susan Marsh is an award-winning writer living in Jackson, Wyoming. She retired from the U.S. Forest Service after thirty years as a wild land steward. After growing up in the forests of the Pacific Northwest, she worked as a geologist, forest manager and naturalist in wild places throughout the western U.S.

With a background in natural science, she has integrated her love of our precious public land with her love of writing to produce several other books, including *War Creek*, *A Hunger for High Country*, *The Wild Wyoming Range*, and *Stories of the Wild*.

Known for her intimate knowledge of the national forest surrounding Jackson Hole, she has introduced many others to its wonders through field trips and workshops. She led the recreation and wilderness program for the Bridger-Teton National Forest between 1988 and 2010, and spent many days working and playing in Cache Creek, the subject of this book. Between 2011 and 2015 she spent over four hundred days in Cache Creek to take photographs and gather information used in the book.

Contact Susan at www.slmarsh.com

Photo: Don Plumley.

Index

Note: For winter wildlife closure information, please refer this book's web page at www.sastrugipress.com for updated links.

Enjoy other Sastrugi Press titles

These Canyons Are Full of Ghosts by Emmett Harder

Driven to find his fortune in the most desolate and forbidding landscapes on earth, one prospector learns there is more to finding gold than just using a shovel and pickaxe. While exploring the massive national park, Emmett Harder crosses paths with Death Valley's most notorious resident: Charles Manson.

Roaming the Wild by Grover Ratliff

Jackson Hole is home to some of the most iconic landscapes in North America. In this land of harsh winters and short summers, wildlife survive and thrive. People from all around the world travel here to savor both the rare vistas of the high Rockies and have the chance to observe bear, moose and elk. It is an environment like no other, covered in snow most of the year yet blanketed by wildflowers for a few precious months. This place is both powerful and delicate.

Antarctic Tears by Aaron Linsdau

What would make someone give up a high-paying career to ski across Antarctica alone? This inspirational true story will make readers both cheer and cry. Fighting skin-freezing temperatures, infections, and emotional breakdown, Aaron Linsdau exposes harsh realities of the world's largest wilderness. Discover what drives someone to the brink of destruction while pursing a dream. Available in print and audiobook formats.

Journeys to the Edge by Randall Peeters, PhD.

Ever wonder what it's like to climb Mount Everest? The idea isn't as far-fetched as it may seem, even though very few people in the world have climbed Mount Everest. It requires dreaming big and creating a personal vision to climb the mountains in your life. Randall Peeters shares his guidelines to create a personal vision.

The Blind Man's Story by J.W. Linsdau

Imagine one's surprise to be hiking in the great Northwest and coming across someone who is blind and spends his summers living high on a mountain. That's what happened to journalist Beau Larson. He returns to work to cover a dispute between local timber workers and environmentalists. Beau finishes his report, but soon discovers there is more to the story than he thought.

Cloudshade by Lori Howe

In every season, life on America's high plains is at once harsh and beautiful, liberating and isolated, welcoming and unforgiving. The poems of *Cloudshade* take us through those seasons, illuminating the intersections between the landscapes surrounding us and those inside us. Extraordinarily relatable, the poems of *Cloudshade* swing wide a door to life in the West, both for lovers of poetry and for those who don't normally read poems. Available in print and audiobook formats.

Voices at Twilight by Lori Howe

The poems, essays, and photographs of *Voices at Twilight* offer the reader a visual tour of a selection of Wyoming's ghost towns. Contained within are travel directions, GPS coordinates, and tips for intrepid readers who wish to experience these unique towns and town sites for themselves. Available in print and audiobook formats.

Visit Sastrugi Press on the web at www.sastrugipress.com to purchase the above titles directly from the publisher. They are also available from your local bookstore or online retailers in print, ebook, or audiobook form. Quantity discounts are available.

Thank you for choosing Sastrugi Press.

www.ingramcontent.com/pod-product-compliance
Lightning Source LLC
Chambersburg PA
CBHW051433270326
41935CB00018B/1819